HOAD
AND OTHER STORIES

Sarah Passingham

First published in 2014
by Stonewood Press
97 Benefield Road, Oundle PE8 4EU
Tel: 0845 456 4838
books@stonewoodpress.co.uk
www.stonewoodpress.co.uk

All rights reserved
Copyright © Sarah Passingham, 2014
The author assert her moral right to be
indentified as the author of this work

ISBN: 978-1-910413-02-9

Distributed by Central Books
99 Wallis Road, London E9 5LN
Email: orders@centralbooks.com
Tel: 0845 458 9911

Printed & bound in the UK by Imprintdigital, Exeter
Designed and typeset in Minion 10.5pt/12.5pt
by www.silbercow.co.uk
Cover illustration by Martin Parker

Acknowledgement: 'Monmouth' first appeared in
Stand: Volume 8 (3), 2008

My thanks to Dennis Passingham, Anna Reckin,
Les Girls Writing Group, Jacqueline Gabbitas and
Martin Parker, The Norwich Writers' Centre, Arts
Council England and to Fred Davies (who sadly
hasn't made it to see these stories published in a
collection) for all their support over the years. – SP

This is the second book in the THUMBPRINT series

Contents

Hoad   5

The Forty-Seven   23

Monmouth   39

For
D, L & M

Hoad

When he came through the door they'd turned their backs on him, leaned their heads together and whispered through suppressed laughter. He'd been in the back room, and they must have stepped over the doormat to prevent the gallery's bell from jangling because it was the sound of their voices that had alerted him.

Hoad stood quite still behind the mahogany table that served as a desk until the pair fell silent and began to stroll around the room.

It was nearly closing time and had been quiet all day. He'd been half way through making a coffee, and wondered if he could go back to it, then decided against. He stood and waited.

'How much?' The boy was pointing at a figurine.

Hoad moved out from behind the table and walked the distance towards them, his footfalls echoing on the limed oak floor, before quoting a sum that was deliberately the high side of accurate. The boy didn't flinch, instead he reached out a hand and caressed the bronze shoulder with his thumb.

Students didn't often come into the gallery. It was several miles from the university, for a start, and those who did venture this far were intimidated by the lack of displayed prices.

'And this?' The boy held out a pale blue lotus bowl.

Hoad, unfailingly polite, named his price and gently retrieved the bowl. The boy nodded and sauntered about the room with his arm around the girl's waist and her hand thrust into the back pocket of his jeans. They moved with a liquid grace as though they were a two-headed mythical animal, the boy always taking the lead. It could have been a dance, with Hoad the single member of an exclusive audience.

He followed at a slight distance and watched them carefully. They stopped beside a large Chinese rug at the far end of the L-shaped room. The boy took his arm from the girl's waist, squatted down and flipped the corner over.

'Silk?'

Hoad nodded.

'It's good.' It was a statement.

'Everything's good,' Hoad said. These two looked like

students – jeans, no coats despite the cold spring, hair that swung loose – but they didn't behave like students.

'How much?' the boy said again.

Hoad had only unpacked the carpet that morning and had thought it perfect, but now he wasn't so sure. He thought there might be some damage to the border, but it could be a trick of the light. 'It's priced at…' he began. He paused for a moment, then gave a figure: it was very expensive. 'But it might be negotiable,' he added.

The boy straightened, took an iPhone from his pocket and moved away. The girl stood still, but ignored the carpet.

Slowly, and with the poise of a performer, she slid her right foot from her shoe and, without looking at Hoad, appeared to admire her pink painted toenails. Caught off guard, Hoad felt momentarily unbalanced.

He quickly glanced over at the boy (her boyfriend or husband, there was no way of telling; neither wore jewellery) but he'd walked almost around the corner at the far end of the gallery and still had his back to them. His one-sided conversation could be heard only as a low murmur. The girl slipped her foot back into its shoe, and only then could Hoad break his gaze to look up at her face. Her eyes were black, almost as black as her hair, which was straight and very long, and was unfathomably lustrous.

He swallowed. His voice, when it emerged, felt like

gravel. 'Is there anything here that you especially like?' he asked.

She pointed to the lit display case against the back wall holding his signature piece – a vase that had cost him his inheritance and won him a global reputation – without, apparently, looking at anything else. 'I've always loved that,' she said. He was confused. He was sure he would have remembered if she had been in the gallery before.

'You have exquisite taste,' he said, and he realised that he'd been holding his breath. 'Do you know what it is?'

She nodded. 'Nephrite jade,' she said with a faint unidentifiable accent. Her voice was so quiet he had to lean towards her until he fancied he could feel the warmth of her body. He'd been on the point of asking her to accompany him over to the case when she turned towards the boy, who had finished his conversation and was gesturing at his watch.

'Tell him to wait,' Hoad said, but the girl took no notice, ran over to her boyfriend and resumed their hip-linked status as they left the gallery.

Through the window, Hoad watched their progress down the street, feeling as frail and hollow as papier-mâché.

For the next three weeks, Hoad arrived at the gallery early and spent every minute waiting for the girl and boy to come back. He changed his routine and spent more time standing looking out of the window, observing the passing cyclists and reflections in the swaying water of the canal. From time to time he walked outside, noting the displays in the other galleries: Kashgai carpets, silks from Thailand, Venetian glass and contemporary paintings. Stopping at an intersection where road and water met, he'd study the shifting patterns of people window shopping, the street-lights shimmering in puddles from the rain.

When the couple hadn't returned at the end of the day following their visit, Hoad had taken the Chinese rug out of the gallery, rolled it up and placed it in the store room. He told his partner that it was imperfect and that he had to contact his supplier before he could set a new price, but he knew he wanted to prevent a sale in case the boy wanted to negotiate.

The days were getting noticeably longer but spring was late and the temperature had, if anything, fallen a couple more degrees. One day, a few unseasonable flurries of snow could be seen beyond the glass. Hoad made the final arrangements for his next buying trip and was looking forward to spending some weeks where the air didn't make him gasp every time he left his front door. He'd already switched off the spotlights, collected his overcoat prior to leaving for the evening and was writing a note to his assistant when the door opened and the girl was standing in the gallery, alone.

Blood rushed through him and he felt everything

from the tips of his fingers to the end of each strand of hair fizz with energy.

'Oh,' she said in her quiet voice. 'You're about to close?'

He let his coat slide to the floor behind the table. 'Not at all,' he said. 'We don't close until six o'clock,' not caring that the discreet sign outside said five-thirty. 'We have…' He revised his words. 'You have nearly thirty-five minutes, at least.'

She walked a few steps into the room and stood motionless, looking at him from those disconcerting black eyes. She'd left the door open, Hoad could feel the freezing air around his feet. Once again the girl wore no coat and he couldn't understand how she could bear to be outside in just a sweater.

'Did you want to see the rug again?' he asked eventually.

'No.'

'Because we still have it, if you were interested.'

'No.' She shook her head slightly and her hair glinted as the movement caused a ripple to move along its length. The palm of his hand tingled with the thought of it.

All at once, she turned on her heel and walked towards the back of the gallery. Hoad sprang forward, shut the door and toyed with locking it – would have put up a 'Closed' sign, if he'd had one – then left it. He followed her to the display case.

'Please, put the light back on,' she said.

Hoad obliged. Immediately the vase inside glowed, not with the green more usually associated with jade, but with a pale, milky translucence, and the structure of the cabinet could be seen faintly through finer sections of the vessel. The girl stood, apparently transfixed for almost a minute. They were standing so close that he could smell her shampoo, and the urge to touch her hair had almost overwhelmed him when she spoke again.

'How much?'

'It's not for sale.' He took a step backwards. Why could people only see things in terms of what they were worth and not what they meant? Too many people came into the gallery with a view to obtaining a good investment that would languish the rest of the owner's life in some vault or safe, unappreciated and unloved.

'I'm pleased.'

The words completely disarmed Hoad. His anger evaporated like mist and curled away into the late afternoon.

'Pleased?'

'Yes. I am glad it's not for sale. It means that it's your favourite piece too.' She paused. 'And I'm glad that it's nephrite. Traditional jade.'

'It would be worth even more if it were jadeite.' Their eyes met in the reflection of the display case. His heart beat rose and rose until the thudding in his throat almost hurt.

'Not to me.' She paused and took a breath. 'Tell me about the vase.'

He turned to look at her. 'Well…' he said, seeing his own eyes reflected in the depths of her black irises, '…you're right. This is my favourite.' He continued without shifting his attention from her face. 'It was this piece that started my passion for Chinese art.'

'That's understandable,' she said, her voice soft. 'Do you know about the vase itself?'

It was difficult to marshal his thoughts but he made himself compose a catalogue description of the vessel. 'It's a Chinese, five-ring, covered dragon vase, probably from the Song Dynasty, carved from a single piece of white jade.' He faltered because his voice seemed on the point of giving out. He observed the flawless texture of her cheek, as smooth as the jade, and how the curve of her lips reflected exactly the upwards curve of the outline of the handles. She nodded for him to continue. He swallowed painfully. 'Each of the rings is part of the original stone but, as you can see, they float loose from the handles, two on the bowl and three on the cover, and the whole is crowned with the head of an imperial dragon.'

The door opened and the bell jangled but he remained staring down at her. 'There is a legend about jade carvers…'

She stepped backwards and waved to someone behind him.

'I'm here,' she called to the boy who was walking

towards them. She looked quickly back at Hoad. 'Tell me the rest of the story next week,' she said and ran the length of the gallery on tip-toe to join the boy. She pulled the door closed behind them.

Hoad cancelled his trip, gave his assistant two weeks holiday and spent every minute of every day of the next week in the gallery. Instead, his partner went to search for antiquities in the sun. The girl did not come back. By Saturday closing time, Hoad began to feel ridiculous; but it didn't stop him staying on in the gallery until past seven o'clock to get the paperwork up to date. By the time he'd set the alarm and left the building he had a plan for the following day.

It had been a long time since he had visited the less fashionable part of the city and he knew a walk that would take him past the picturesque canals of the old town, on the outskirts of which lay the university. Spring was at last emerging from her winter sleep. The blossom that had been nothing but a pink haze outline on the branches in the early part of the week had now burst through with an exuberance of buds and scent. Bird song filled the air and Hoad felt the sun warm his cheeks for the first time in months.

And with the sun came the students. They crowded the wooden seats beside the canal-side bars. They sat heaped together in a bundle of scarves and sweaters on every available surface, laughing and drinking.

Hoad walked the towpath and scanned their faces. Sometimes he saw a skein of black hair but it never had quite the lustre he was looking for. Occasionally there was something about the way someone walked, and once he thought he heard her voice but when he turned his head, a coarse-looking girl, tipped her chin up and laughed. Always he was disappointed. He wished he had a dog with him but he made the glorious day his excuse for extended exercise. He bought a drink and something to eat and joined the throng at the wooden tables for an hour. His feet hurt and his back ached but he was curiously happy. Some of the wild irresponsibility of his companions had infected his usually impenetrable seriousness. By dusk – his mission a failure, as he knew it must be – he turned away from the student quarter and headed back towards his own comfortable apartment building.

He was less than a block away from his destination when he saw her.

On the far side of the road was a coffee bar. The windows were illuminated with the lamps set out on tables within and, although the glass was clouded in a half-moon of condensation, he clearly saw her profile turned towards him.

He stepped into the road and walked straight across, not registering the angry blast from a passing car. On the pavement he stood facing her where she sat looking out into the street. Looking at him.

He smiled and lifted a gloved hand in salutation before turning to the entrance. Inside, the heat and conversation was like a stockade preventing him from seeing her. He ordered an espresso at the counter and, in a sudden burst of ambition, two slices of Genoa cake. After an agonisingly slow transaction, he picked up his cup and, balancing the two plates in one hand, he negotiated the shifting crowd of people taking refuge from the evening chill.

When he looked up from the swirling coffee and maze of bentwood chairs, smile already prepared, she was nowhere to be seen.

Desperately he searched the space towards the door, but she'd vanished. How had she walked past without him noticing? But she had acknowledged him; was expecting him with his offering of cake and myth. Bewildered and abandoned he looked across at the table where she had sat and saw with a shock that the view to the street was black. The pavement, between pools of light from the street lamps, was quite opaque through the steam and darkness. A one-way mirror only. She couldn't have seen him at all.

On Monday morning, Hoad cursed his impulsiveness in giving the gallery assistant the extra holiday. She was due only a single week and letting her have extra days for no real reason meant that he had no choice but to open the gallery himself. He dressed with the care that he always took. His suit was perfectly pressed. Only his tie jarred. It had been a present and was one he didn't wear often. He didn't like the pattern, which was taken from a painting by Klimt and too obvious for his taste, but he chose it purposely and as a personal statement that marked the end of an unusually foolish episode of his life.

The girl came into the gallery at midday. Hoad was almost annoyed to see her.

'Can I help you?' he asked, as he would any visitor.

She hesitated and her glance flicked backwards towards the street outside. She regained her composure and walked forwards a step or two. 'You were going to tell me about the jade carver,' she said.

Hoad wondered if he might say something about seeing her in the café. Or if she would. But then he remembered that she hadn't seen him.

Together they walked towards the display case and the vase. It was lit artificially from above and the sunshine from the windows highlighted small honey-coloured inclusions in the three feet supporting the bowl. It looked as beautiful as the first time he had seen it in the house of the man who was to become his business partner. It had cost all he had at the time but he felt he was buying a piece of Chinese history, part of an ancient culture that had captured his soul, like seeing something living within the stone itself.

'Jade, as I am sure you know...' He smiled to

acknowledge her previous comments and his heart leaped as she smiled in return, opening her mouth a little so that he could see the rosy tip of her tongue, '...is an exceptionally hard stone. Nephrite jade is softer than some but has a grain which calls for great skill from the carver.' He grazed her elbow to turn her aside so that he could lift the lid of a small glass-topped table, but then found himself unable to release his contact with her. He saw a muscle move in her cheek and she lifted her arm free. He spoke quickly to cover his embarrassment. 'Even a small piece like this,' he gave her a carved chimaera to hold, avoiding her fingers as he did so, 'will take many hours and many years of experience. You cannot chip or chisel jade. Every piece must be worn away either by abrasion with tools or sand pastes.' He felt he was losing her attention. 'Think of the inside of a feather-thin bowl...'

'But the carver, tell me about the carver,' she said.

Perhaps he could invite her to lunch. He could lock up the gallery for an hour or two and he would have time to tell her the legend of the jade carver whose design was like an autograph in every piece he touched and who fell in love with his patron's daughter, carving his pieces solely for her. They would share a bottle of wine and he could settle into the tale and she would listen with her eyes glistening as he revealed the last fatal line of the story.

The bell jangled and immediately Hoad thought the

boy had returned to reclaim his girlfriend, but it was a group of three customers who had a history of making infrequent, but significant purchases.

'Excuse me. I must see to this,' he said but he left the lid of the table open as a token of his trust.

Hoad could tell immediately the men were not in a serious investment mood but had come to see what was new. They split up and wandered around the gallery looking at everything and nothing. He had to be attentive. At one point the girl walked back to the entrance and Hoad broke off his conversation to intercept her.

'I'm sure they won't be long,' he said.

'I have to go now.'

'I'd like to finish telling you the story.'

'Would you let me hold the vase?'

'Would you have lunch with me?' he said, which was no answer.

She was silent for a moment and moved nearer the door. Hoad expected to see the boy there but the street was empty and only the shop canopies flicked in the breeze.

'Can I hold the vase?' she repeated. Her eyes caught him again.

'What's your name?' He had to be quick, the man whose conversation he'd broken was getting impatient and was walking towards them.

'Ting. Ting Ting Yu Li. Will you let me hold the vase?'

'Come back in an hour and we'll have lunch, Ting Ting Yu Li.' Hoad opened the door and waited for her to leave. She remained where she was, and Hoad's customer paused, looking uneasily between the two. She was waiting for her question to be answered. Hoad stood by the open door.

'Maybe,' he said. Then, suddenly reckless, 'Yes.'

For the rest of the day there was an unusual flurry of activity in the gallery and Hoad was kept occupied answering queries, taking contacts and, once, making a sale. It was nearly two hours before the girl returned and, as though in answer to a prayer, the last customer left as she slipped in through the open door.

When Hoad looked up and saw her, he feared he might teeter and had to clutch the edge of his desk to steady himself. He'd been very busy but he'd found the time to disarm the alarm to the display case, certain that she would be back, and the key was already in his pocket. He slipped his hand in and jutted the sharp edge into his palm as he walked towards her. He hadn't opened the case in fifteen years.

'I haven't booked but there's a good restaurant in the next street that I'm sure would still be open.' he said.

'I've eaten.'

'Oh,' said Hoad.

'You said I could hold the vase.'

'I said "maybe".'

He noticed that uncertain flicker of her eyes towards the door again, then she smiled, took his hand in her soft cool fingers and led him towards the back of the gallery.

It was so long since he'd held the vase in his hands he had forgotten how cold it was. It was small, just fifteen centimetres high and little more at the widest part of the bowl. It was completely unmarked: perfect, just as it had been when it had left the carver's hand.

'This vessel,' said Hoad to the girl, 'is probably a thousand years old. Chinese wisdom says that "Gold has a value, but jade is priceless". It was believed to be a link between the physical and spiritual worlds, and has been prized as long as Chinese civilisation itself.' A smile softened his eyes, 'But you already know that.' He put the vase down on a table beside them, then turned to the girl and, unable to prevent his voice from trembling said, 'Jade to jade, Ting Ting Yu Li.'

She held out her hands towards the vase. Hoad closed her fingers around the ringed handles and covered them with his palms. They stood looking at each other over the up-tilted head of the dragon and he felt her fingers flutter under his own.

'I want to see the translucence in daylight,' she said. 'I want to see what's inside.' Then she walked the length of the gallery and around the L, towards the front windows. The boy came inside and the bell jangled. He held the door open for her and she walked out into the street, stepping over the doormat as she did so, holding the vase high in front of her with the confidence of a priestess.

Hoad watched her every movement from beside the empty display case: every step, every blink of her eye, every shift of her fingers on the white jade bowl. Ting Ting Yu Li walked a few steps parallel with the gallery window to move from the shadow of the awning into the sunlight, directly in front of Hoad. She moved the vase with its five floating rings slowly away from her body until she was standing with it held at arms' length over the expanse of grey, hard concrete. She turned to look at him through the glass, looked away, then back, her face as impassive as the surface of the jade.

NOTE: Ting ting yu li in Pinyin translates as 'slim and graceful'. Ting ting means 'beautiful and nice'. Yu means 'jade'. Li has a number of meanings, including 'stay alive or upright' and is occasionally used as a family name.

The Forty-Seven

Ray Norveg squinted between the strands of ivy and examined the men approaching his house. There were two of them and they were on foot.

Ray couldn't remember the last time he'd had visitors but it must be over twenty years. He drew back from the window and leaned against the wall, sucked air deep into his lungs and forced himself to look again.

The sun hung high in the sky and the men dripped sweat as they slashed at the vegetation with switches cut from the hedge. Giant hogweed, alkenet and Japanese knotweed obstructed the way. Here and there a bramble patch threatened to halt their path completely. Thistles plucked at shirts that hung limply on their soft white bodies, and nettles standing shoulder high in the summer heat made vicious attacks on their hands and faces. Most of the plants had claimed the driveway for themselves but from time to time Ray had added his own treasures to ensure his privacy.

But still they came closer.

Fear glittered in Ray's eyes and the bones of his face stood out from his quivering skin like the frame of a tent.

He raised his head and sniffed. The air was thick with frustration and impatience. For a split second he stood frozen, then turned and bolted up the stairs. At the half-landing he gave a low whistle to call the other occupants in the house, then he scurried to the top.

The men emerged from the neglected driveway into a weedy clearing. Ray could hear swearing and puffing through the broken window panes. He beckoned to the others to follow him and they moved into the room above the front door. Ray kneeled on the floor, put his hands on the windowsill and pulled himself up so that he had a view of the ground.

Somebody rapped loudly on the door. Ray trembled, folded his arms over his head and waited. The others crept closer.

'Hey! Anybody at home?' A moment's quiet. 'Hello-o-o. Anybody there?' More soft talk, then silence.

After a while, Ray looked through the window again. The men were crawling around the base of the walls. Ray saw them poking twigs down holes and filling little plastic tubes with things they found on the ground. He heard the back door rattle, but Ray never left the doors unbolted and he held his breath until the men gave up. They walked round his house for nearly half an hour, then they went away down the verdurous drive.

Ray watched them until they had vanished from sight and all stalks of vegetation had stopped moving. A hot green quiet, pricked by the hum of honey bees, descended on the building. He waited some more, and, only when he was absolutely certain he was not about to be disturbed again, did he walk downstairs to prepare his meal. He shared it, as always, scrupulously fairly, ensuring that not one greedy appetite was sated before the others.

Ten days later, the men came back. This time Ray was out. He returned on the back road, wheeling his bicycle through the copse until he came to a ruined piggery hidden by brambles. He pushed his bike under the shelter of a corrugated iron roof then, dropping almost to his knees, negotiated the tunnels in the undergrowth, familiar with constant use, at a trot.

He saw the sign on the door immediately.

He stood in front of this evidence of invasion and began to shake. All at once little feet pattered over his boots, warm bodies pressed his legs, and when he looked down he saw concern in their sharp black eyes.

With a howl he lunged forward and wrenched the

notice from his door. He tried to rip it apart but it was laminated and wouldn't tear. He punched it into the wall again and again until the plastic cracked. He ground brick dust into the surface so that the words were unreadable then he spun it from his hand like a spiked discus so that it was lost from sight in the pheasant copse.

He stood breathing hard, then, remembering something forgotten in the enormity of the moment, he reached into his pocket and pulled out two abandoned multicoloured pets, sprung from the animal shelter where he worked. Held in the palm of one bloodied hand he stroked the fine hair of these latest particular favourites: a curly-haired Rex and a Topaz. He straightened out their naked tails, felt their whiskers shiver against his lips and cooed at them as a mother would her baby. With great tenderness he set them down on the ground amongst the other rats.

Ray tried to forget what he had seen but the words CONDEMNED and UNFIT crammed his waking moments. At night he had nightmares filled with bulldozers and wrecking balls. At work he carried out his duties as usual. During the second week after finding the notice, Ray returned to the house to discover a letter had been pinned to his door. It was a notice to quit.

Ray was fifty-two years old. He'd lived in the house

all his life. After his father died, the Estate owners had been happy for Ray to take over the tenancy and he lived alone for the next twenty-five years. I'm too old to start looking for somewhere else, he excused himself but in his heart he knew that ordinary folk would think his habits strange. That evening he started to move his few belongings into the piggery.

By chance, it wasn't one of Ray's days for the shelter on the morning that the man from the Council came to visit, or the outcome might have been even more devastating. He'd been expecting to hear heavy machinery as a prelude to what was to come. Instead he was tending his vegetable patch at the back of the house when all he heard was footsteps, so he hid. Too late he realised what was happening and by the time he was able to remove the trays of poisoned grain, several dozen of his sharp-faced companions had enjoyed a feast.

The weekend was almost over before the first tell-tale signs appeared, but Ray had remained vigilant throughout, barely dozing, and alert to any signals of distress from his family. When first one, then another and another stretched out unnaturally from their usual curled up sleeping position, Ray opened his eyes wide and watched with a fierce concentration.

Blue shadows spread deep under the leaves, but as the moonlight changed to dawn, the rusted corrugated iron roof of his father's old pigsty let through light enough to see that the tight bundle of sleeping rodents lay broken and ragged. Those on the margins of the nest opened their mouths exposing long teeth that showed black in the emerging day, from time-to-time the silence was broken by a gasp for breath or a fretful whimper. Ray saw the rich golden fawn of his newly acquired Topaz at the very edge, and frowned when a tremor ran the length of its spine.

He leaned over and stroked the silken fur from between translucent ears to pale pink snout. The tip felt fevered and dry beneath his touch. Then, with a slight movement that Ray took to be resignation, blood began to ooze from the corner of a barely twitching nostril – a viscous sludge marring that once spotless and shimmering muzzle.

From the artful, undomesticated rats that populated the runs and tunnels around his house, to the impish fancy rats he liberated from the shelter, Ray loved all the brothers. But, despite his quest for fairness, not all his love was equal. The golden-coated Topaz had taken to sitting in the crook of his arm, and Ray imagined relaxing after his evening meal without that warming smudge against his body.

Quiet and relentless, death was inevitable, but only after every drop of blood had ruptured into body cavities, leaked from naked ears, stained whiskers. If he left the poison to take its slow and painful course, eventually they would all be steeped in gore.

Ray forced the knuckles of one hand into his mouth to stifle a rising grief. Or perhaps it was anger. Whichever it was, if he was going to do this properly, he couldn't allow himself to give in to emotion yet. When he was certain beyond doubt that he knew which of his brood were dying and not simply sleeping, he reached out a comforting hand to each suffering creature in turn and lifted it away from the nest. Feeling for exactly the right place beneath each skull, he lovingly but swiftly wrung its neck. With each crack of the fragile bones, he gave into his anguish a little more.

At dawn, and weeping openly by this time, he smoothed the soil to make an area free of stones, and laid out his dead. After choosing a spot away from the high ground where the piggery was situated, but that wouldn't get waterlogged, he dug a small grave, lined it with sprigs of crushed rosemary to keep the foxes away, and buried the little bodies. Forty seven in all. One pale coloured corpse glowed gold and shining in the early morning rays.

The surviving rats stood a few yards off, wary whiskers twitching in alarm. At midday, they did not join Ray to share his meal. Outrage came with the force of a lightning strike, not directed at the rest of the brothers – Ray couldn't blame their sudden caution – but unequivocally aimed at those who had violated his way of life.

At the shelter, the talk was all about changes on the Estate. Ray never joined in the gossip but he couldn't help overhearing the rumours.

The burden of anger and grief that he was carrying made it difficult to undertake his duties. Each rodent tank took him twice as long as usual to clean out. He felt compelled to pick up each rat and check it minutely for signs of ill health. He felt their whiskers flit across his face, breathed in their musky, earth smell and gazed into eyes as bright and hard as beads of jet. He longed to set them free.

Two families came that day to offer new homes.

'Rats are sociable creatures,' he blurted out, alarming himself and the kennel maid who was walking past. 'You can't just leave them in a cage like mice or they'll destroy each other. You must occupy them.'

'Oh, yes', said the man easily; the woman hung back. 'We've had rats before. Our Lenny has them in his bedroom.'

Ray looked at Lenny. Lenny looked back owlishly, eyes huge behind round spectacles. He reached into the tank and allowed a black male to crawl up his arm and onto his shoulder. It sat up on its hind legs and washed its face. Lenny winked at Ray and Ray felt a surge of jealously.

It was never quite the same again. Ray sat outside the pigsties when it was fine, and under the corrugated iron roof when it was not. The nights were drawing in but Ray was oblivious to the cold. The rats were happy to share his food again as always, but they took it beyond his arm's reach to eat it. They didn't share his blanket or gambol around his feet as he gardened. The bond had been broken and it seemed it couldn't be repaired. Ray's sense of fairness was insulted. He had killed the brothers not from malice but out of compassion; nevertheless a rat cannot understand motive, he can only see the result.

Nearly three months passed before the bulldozers arrived so it was a shock when they did. It had been weeks since he had set foot in the house and, so used to the outdoors had he become, he realised that apart from the earth-shattering noise of the bricks collapsing, he hardly cared. He gave up shaving, swam in the ornamental lake when he felt uncomfortable, and never washed his clothes. When his boot sole came away from the upper he didn't bother to get it repaired but threw the pair away, so it was hardly surprising when the shelter manager called him into her office one day.

'Ray, you know I hold you in the greatest respect,' she said. 'I've never had a more experienced or devoted rodent superintendent and it pains me to have to speak to you like this.' She furrowed her brow. 'We've received complaints.' She waited for him to make a comment. He remained silent squinting at his filth-covered feet.

'You're obviously in some kind of trouble or you wouldn't come to work, even at an animal shelter, in this degree of...' She looked upwards as though she would find the word she was looking for written above his head somewhere. She found it and thrust it at him. '...dishevelment. You're going to have to clean yourself up or I'll have to let you go.'

Ray met her eye, a unique occurrence, raised both hands to his long nose and delicately rubbed at it with his forefingers. 'I've been evicted,' he said.

'Evicted! Why?'

Ray shrugged his shoulders.

'Did you fall behind with your rent?'

'No.'

'They should have offered you alternative accommodation or notice to find somewhere else.'

'I didn't know.' Ray pulled at his ear. 'Thirty days notice. They said the place was condemned, unfit for human habitation.'

She snorted. 'It's their responsibility to ensure that buildings don't fall into disrepair.' She told him his rights, said that tenants all over the estate were being thrown out by the new landlord. The animal shelter itself had received notice of a huge rent increase. She offered to bring him an information leaflet the next day but Ray shook his head and made his excuses. She was kind, but she reminded him of her ultimatum.

Back in the rodent house he didn't hesitate. He

found an old feed sack without holes and systematically went from tank to tank decanting the occupants. Then he took the writhing bag and climbed onto his bicycle.

The anger within him expanded so that by the time he reached the crossroads he felt that he might explode. He'd lost his family home, forty-seven of his companions, the trust of the rest of the pack, and his job. This wasn't playing by the rules. He didn't deserve any of it. He bent his head into the breeze and pedalled hard past his wood towards the big hall at the end of the village.

It hadn't crossed Ray's mind that the Estate owner might have a wife and children. Hidden behind the summer house, his bicycle left pushed into a hedge at the bottom of the drive, he looked on at the young family playing in their garden. The children were tow-haired and bronzed from a foreign holiday. They wore brightly coloured fleeces against the chill of the autumn day and shouted with excitement as a tennis ball flew high into the air. A terrier darted between their feet trying to intercept the ball on its curving path. Ray glanced down at the sack at his feet; small movements and rummages disturbed the surface of the fabric. He looked at the side door that lay enticingly ajar, then again at the family in the garden, but humanity prevailed.

'Come on,' he whispered. 'This isn't right. An eye for an eye and all. But only an eye for an eye. No more. The wife and kids are innocent.' He slipped back through the gap in the hedge to where his bicycle was waiting and dropped his sack gently into the basket. 'And I can't risk you in that house when there's a dog about.'

Ray paused before setting off, having a sudden thought. 'And anyway, they'd probably use poison again.' It was too soon, he needed time before making a proper decision. 'We'll have to do better than this,' he said under his breath as he swung his leg over the back wheel, then spent the return journey planning how he would introduce such a large number of shelter rats into his home pack.

Autumn came and the long Indian summer remained only as headlines on the tabloid newspapers that wrapped fish and chips bought from the town, eaten in a lay-by near Ray's pheasant copse and abandoned by the side of the road. Gales stripped the deciduous woodland of cover and exposed the roof of the piggery to clattering rain. The bulldozers completed their devastation and left. A three metre high chain-link fence prevented Ray from visiting the site of his old house and soon the whole countryside was unrecognisable as the area was re-landscaped in preparation for a new golf course and country club.

Ray watched for the newspapers and scoured them clean of uneaten chips and battered fish-skin. In the vegetable patch he abandoned the gardening tools and used his hands instead. He left potatoes and carrots in the ground and ate them as he needed them, raw and earth-brown. Water from the puddles took on a new piquancy and windfall apples were a sumptuous treat.

His bicycle was abandoned and rusty with lack of use, lying where it had fallen during a winter storm. The tunnels in the woodland became rat-runs to the edges of other people's gardens where he and the brothers would find dustbins to scavenge. Forgotten caches of vegetables and the occasional bird, dead from lack of food or the bitter cold, provided enough to keep the pack alive all through the winter. The lake never quite froze over so there was always fresh water and, despite the bone-chilling weather, Ray still enjoyed a regular swim. The cold had never bothered him. He examined the dark hair that grew on his forearms and observed how it had thickened and lengthened; now he curled up with his liberated brothers and felt snug and content. His nails, uncut, had grown hard and curved and his senses sharper and more focused. He began to forget what it must have been like to live in a house. He became cunning, opportunistic and, above all, unscrupulous.

In the early summer, the golf course opened to a few elite players and work began on a beach area to turn the shallow lake into a centre for water sports. The rats were not afraid of much but they kept away from the earth movers and tractors during the day. After dusk there were rich pickings to be had from the contractors' rubbish but Ray resented the desecration of his tranquil lake. The water became tainted and the reed beds defiled. The wildfowl moved away and the water lilies died.

Then Ray became ill.

The work went on at the lakeside and Ray sweated with fever. He imagined he was back in the house watching the men from the Environmental Health Department cut their way through the jungle. The earth movers left for another job. Ray hallucinated that his father fed him bitter herbs and cool water in a nutshell. The builders completed the lakeside chalet. Ray's kidneys scorched in a blaze of pain.

On the day that Ray awoke, blessedly cool but grass-stem weak, the first bathers and canoeists took to the water. He heard their shrieks of laughter from the wood and began to recall something from his encyclopaedic knowledge of rats.

That evening he dragged himself down to the water's edge for a long desired and deeply refreshing swim. He encouraged the brothers to follow and one by one they slipped into the moonlit water and played.

The air was mild; away from the artificial beach, yellow-green willow tendrils stroked the grassy banks and Ray sat in the shallows drinking and drinking the water. When the rats had wandered sleepily back to the pheasant copse, Ray stood by himself at the edge of the water and considered the numbers of people who would flock to enjoy the leisure facilities offered by the new owner of the estate. He swam into his lake and, quite deliberately, relieved his bursting bladder into the water.

The chain link fencing went up almost four weeks to the day. Ray felt fully recovered. He sauntered down to the edge of the golf course to watch the contractors, a satisfied smile hovering around his whiskers. The workers were taking a break and eating chips from a newspaper. The smell made Ray's mouth water. He crept a little closer.

The men leapt toward Ray. But he had got what he wanted and seen the headlines on the newspapers. *Forty seven deaths from Rat Fever. Weil's Disease closes new Leisure Lake.*

Ray turned his back on the men and, from the safety of the wood, he washed his face carefully before rejoining his brothers in the pheasant copse. Forty-seven. There were bound to be more, although he couldn't help that. He was satisfied.

Monmouth

He has me waiting again.

It is the privilege of the disabled to have people waiting. Only I mustn't call him disabled. I mustn't call him anything. Not paraplegic. Not invalid – he is far from invalid. Not legless – though he is, on occasions that warrant it, drunk. Not handicapped. Not victim. Definitely not victim.

I could now, though. I could call him anything I like; now he can't answer back. But I won't. His fear stays in me like letters through a stick of rock. And like sticks of rock we'll shatter under stress. We don't like change. He didn't like change. Keep everything facing the same way, the way we have always done and we'll be all right.

The corridor is over-lit and featureless. Two seats wait side by side. I occupy one, the other is empty.

There's only me now. The others grabbed their lives and ran with them years ago. I'm still waiting for mine. I'll have waited forty-one years next Saturday. A few more hours won't hurt.

A woman materialises beside me and smiles kindly. 'Sorry for the wait. There was an urgent legal-aid case. Would you like a cup of tea?'

'Thanks. Black,' I say. He didn't like milk. Wouldn't have it in the house. Thought it would give him tuberculosis.

'It's all pasteurised, now,' I'd say.

'Piffle. That's what you think. They leave an inch of formaldehyde in the bottom of the churn to make it last longer. Rots your kidneys.'

'Tankers, they use tankers. No one's used churns for years,' I said.

'Think you're so bloody smart,' he said.

I did, actually. I was smart. Could have got to university, Miss Harrison said. But Mum abandoned her marriage vows, went off with the local pig farmer and moved to Wales. A crying shame, Miss Harrison said. I told Mum if it was pigs she wanted, she could have stayed at home. She said, less of your lip and clipped me round the ear. Then she hugged me and whispered sorry. I wasn't sure if she was sorry for clouting me or sorry for leaving me with him.

'You ought to get out more,' I'd said.

'More! What do you mean more?'

'Well. At all.'

'What the hell do I want to be going out there for?' I noticed his knuckles blanch on the arms of his chair.

'You might like it.'

'I don't.'

'I could take you to the pictures, or maybe you could just sit in the garden, smell the flowers.'

'Sod the flowers.'

'Well, the cinema, then. You'd like that.'

'I've been to the cinema. I went with your mother in 1962.'

'There's been a few films made since then.'

'Saw that Cubby Broccoli thing – *Dr No*. That wasn't a film, that was a road crash.'

'It's good. I saw that on the telly.'

'You don't know what you're talking about.'

'What is good then, Dad?' He always had an opinion.

'*The Third Man*. That's good. *Casablanca*, *The Maltese Falcon*, *Double Indemnity*, *Crossfire*. Those are films worth wasting time on.'

He had a point. About the quality of the films, not my lack of knowledge. I never did tell him about me doing Media Studies; he would have laughed till he choked.

'*The Third Man* to *Dr No*. That's quite a jump there, Dad,' I said. 'Thirteen years is a lot of time to lose.'

'I didn't lose it. It lost me.'

'Let me get you a television, Dad. You're missing so much,' I said.

'And you think seeing what I'm missing will make me feel better?'

What he really wanted was a son. And in the end, he got one. My baby brother, seven years my junior. Weed and wastrel but, oh so charming. Went west with our mother and the pig farmer while I stayed put to keep the home fires burning. Then at sixteen he put on a spurt of growth and maturity. Grew to six-feet two inches, got his head down and worked. Went to university in Manchester and specialised in engineering like Dad but didn't make it to work with the big boys. He married an accountant from Cardiff; it broke Dad's heart when they could only produce daughters.

The tea arrives. It's milky and lukewarm. In an identical corridor in a parallel universe, someone is peering into my hot, black tea and wondering what happened to the milk. I push the cup under the other chair and pretend I haven't seen it.

'Mike to see you, Dad.'

'Good of you to drop by,' as if a trip of three hundred miles could be said to be dropping by.

Now that his friends from the old days were wrinkled and lame he resumed contact.

'Got something here that might be of interest.'

'Doubt it,' he said.

Three hours later they'll still be poring over engine parts and thumbing through manuals to find the code number for a replacement.

'Phil to see you, Dad.'

'Good God! Where'd you spring from?'

'Got something that might be of interest.'

'Doubt it,' he said.

'It gets you upstairs without having to leave your wheelchair.'

'Sod off,' he said and turned his face to the wall for two whole days.

'I've got someone I'd like you to meet, Dad.' I'd waited six months for this moment.

'Oh yes?'

'Dad, meet Brian. Brian, this is my dad.'

'Pleased to meet you, sir.'

'She hasn't told you about me, then.'

'Oh, she has. All about you.'

'Really?' He took a last drag of his cigarette before stubbing it out. 'Brian! What sort of a name is that, Brian? You a social worker? Come to see if we're living up to scratch, have you? Make sure she microwaves the chicken chasseur until it's piping hot and irons my underpants?'

'No.'

'Oh, I see. You want to see I don't pee the bed too often, expose myself at the window or throw turds at the neighbour's dog?'

'No, really...'

'I know your sort. Checking up on us. Brian! Are you Welsh?' He glanced at me to see that he was having the desired effect. And he was.

'You'll want to count the whisky bottles by the bin? Not all mine, you know. She drinks it as well,' he said.

Have to, Dad. Keeps me sane.

'Where are we? Thursday. You'll find three, four? Maybe five on a good week. Come on. Come on, girl. Get the glasses. Let Brian join us, see if we can crack another.' I'd planned a different sort of celebration.

'Leaving already? Bit too much for you, am I? Not lost my marbles, have I? Got all my chairs at home. Well, I've got this one at least.'

'I think I'd better go now.'

'Go on, then. Bugger off. Tell your boss I'm as fit as a fiddle. I've only got one lung and two legs that are about as useful as a fart in a colander, but I'm perfectly healthy.' He may not have been able to walk but he was really in his stride by now and nothing was going to stop him. Not even Brian backing out of the room.

'And while you're about it, tell him to order another Everest & Jennings. Zimmer wheelchairs are crap. Put together by housewives. Those designed by the

Americans, Everest & Jennings, now there's a bit of engineering.'

Then he opened the window and yelled into the garden he wouldn't sit in. 'Couldn't have done better myself.' The first and only time he referred to his pre-accident days.

'Too bloody small, that's what's wrong with this one.' He shifted uncomfortably on his Supasoft gel cushion as though to prove a point, then raised his voice again as Brian climbed into the car. 'Life is better with a Zimmer! Isn't that what the advert says in your social worker handout? Life is crap with a Zimmer! Life without a Zimmer is what we're after. Remember that.'

'What did he want? He never said.'
'No.'
'Oh well, he'll be back. They always are.'
'I doubt it. Drink your whisky, Dad.'

I'm hot and thirsty. I look at my watch. Fifty minutes. Not long by my standards. It used to take fifty minutes to get Dad dressed after he washed himself at the basin in his bedroom. Slap, slap, slap went the flannel under his arms and flecks of soap would stick to the wallpaper and the mirror. Couldn't stand the thought that he might whiff. He insisted on taking a bath twice a week – nearly two hours from start to finish. On his back, a scar of fifty-six stitches carved in a half-moon from shoulder to waist where they'd removed his lung in the year that *Dr. No* was made. Fifteen minutes to negotiate the stairs. He would lift his weight onto his arms as I carried his legs then pushed a cushion under his backside by sleight-of-hand as he lifted himself onto the next tread. Dad called it boggatting. I called it bloody hard work. We arrived in the hall in a lather of sweat and name-calling.

Dad had a thing about names; said he'd chosen ours with great care. My brother finally returned from Wales with a wife and family, presented them with a flourish and proudly introduced them all.

'Angharad and Bronwen!' Dad whacked the arms of his chair. 'What sort of names are those?'

The children burst into tears.

'Beautiful names,' I said and reached for my baby niece to rock her in my arms.' Not Charles, I thought. Not even George.

Gwyneth told me she wouldn't come again. 'He's uncouth, your father. Doesn't just carry one chip but has the whole forest on his shoulder, I reckon. Am I right?' she'd said.

I call Monmouth and speak to my nieces regularly just to remind them that they have a bit of family this side of the country. Sometimes they send me postcards or drawings. Angharad must be nearly nine by now.

'Mr Gibson's ready for you now.'

'Thank you,' I say and follow her into an office. I don't think she's seen the tea cup. Mr Gibson rises to his feet with difficulty due to his size and approaches me with hand outstretched. It's wide and fleshy; the nails are stained with nicotine and dirty. Hard to see what Dad saw in him. He invites me to sit down and apologises for keeping me waiting.

'It's no problem,' I say truthfully. I have only to toe the line for a few more days. To be honest, I don't hold any great hopes for the outcome of this appointment and I shall be surprised if there is anything for me. Dad was so obsessed about carrying on the family name… and I realise, with a jolt, that this is the reason my brother, his only son, the one who could only produce daughters, hasn't turned up. Mr Gibson shuffles the papers – I swear he's arranging his face ready for another apology – as he presses his bulk back into his chair.

'Now, the question of your father's will…' The telephone buzzes, he picks it up with a sigh then leaves the room.

I wait. The room is green and beige, smells of yesterday's cigarettes and there's an ink stain to the left of his desk. It reminds me of a map of Wales.

It's been over a week since the noise in the bedroom. A week since I drove forty miles north and gave my aunt – his sister – the news in person. 'That's the best news I've had all day,' she'd said. 'What a way to go! I hope I keel over and kick the bucket all in the space of a few seconds.' I looked at her over a slice of seedy cake and nodded; she wouldn't last five minutes in a home. Neither would he. A week since I called my brother and told him.

'It wasn't unexpected,' he'd said. But, somehow, I hadn't seen it coming.

For those seven days I cleaned and washed and scrubbed; made the place presentable for after the funeral. Well, I had the time now. So much time. 'What are you going to do?' my brother asked. He'd come without Gwyneth and the girls, but he showed me some snaps. I looked across at Dad's sister. 'Don't you dare. I'm fine on my own,' she said. And I took it to heart.

The stain by the desk spreads in a line from Holyhead, Caernarfon, and points with an inky finger towards Bardsey Island. In my head, I trace the edge through Aberystwyth, Cardigan and Fishguard. I recognise Swansea, Cardiff and float up the Bristol Channel to Monmouth. I've never seen Monmouth.

I reach into my bag to fish out the pictures my brother gave me, and slip them out of the envelope that I'd put them in to keep them nice. Bronwen stands feet astride a red trike that's a little too big for her. Angharad has pigtails and a wayward fringe that reminds me of my own. There are others; family photos taken down by the river.

After that, things get a bit hazy.

As I'm on my way out, the woman sees me through an open door, smiles and says, 'Not long now.'

I'd forgotten there was a river. 'I'm going,' I say. 'I've waited too long.'

The cup of tea is still on duty, where I left it.

END

SARAH PASSINGHAM has published four books of non-fiction and a libretto. Her short stories have appeared in journals including *The London Magazine*, *Brittle Star* and *Stand Magazine*, and in the anthology *Said and Done* (Stonewood Press, 2011). Her work has also been broadcast by the BBC. She won the Julia Fitzgerald Award for short fiction 1996. Her family memoir is nearing completion.

www.sarahpassingham.co.uk